CLIMB
Your Own
LADDER

Become the CEO of
Your Own Business

DANA MALSTAFF

Paperback ISBN: 978-0-9970451-2-3

Cover Design: Fresh Design
Editing: Sheri Roque
Author Photo: Taylor Barker

CONTENTS

PART 1: The Ladder Principle

PART 2: Creating Your Ladder

PART 3: The Steps On Your Ladder

PART 4: Troubleshooting

WANT FREE SUPPORT
WHILE YOU CLIMB?

You don't have to grow your online business alone. We have great free resources to help you make the climb.

Go to www.climbyourownladder.com for all of the resources mentioned in this book, as well as exclusive access to a free training that walks you through how 7-fugure online businesses are structured.

PART 1

THE LADDER
PRINCIPLE

The beginning is the most important part of the work.

Plato

1

How The Ladder Analogy Came To Be

When you have an online business, you end up talking a lot and creating a lot of content. You're continually trying to figure out your unique voice, ideas, and way of thinking to help your voice get heard among the growing masses of people who are trying to do the same thing. This is not a book about creating content, and it's not a book about how to get your voice heard. "Climb Your Own Ladder" is field guide that shows you the natural progression you will make as you grow your business. The idea hit me one day while I was chugging along recording a podcast episode. Yep, it was one of those ah-ha moments.

As for me, I'm not so good at scripting things out before I jump in and get started. I'm more of the just hit record and start talking kind of gal. I like the way my brain thinks when it has some space to roam free, simply because new exciting things are born when I don't confine myself. Sometimes that means I need to edit, but I would much rather edit something that didn't work than never know the fantastic idea or analogy that might have come to life.

On this particular day, I believe we were talking about the stress of owning your own business and being the boss. I love a good analogy, so without even thinking I mentioned that you don't get to start at the top of your ladder. The several minute rant that followed attempted to make the point that we put an immeasurable amount of stress on ourselves when we start an online business, trying to run it like a CEO would, but that's just not how it works. We have to climb each step and earn our way to the top. So stop beating yourself up over not feeling like the

CEO you envisioned yourself to be and allow yourself to be where you are. The sooner you give yourself permission to climb your ladder, the sooner you will free up your mind and capabilities to move forward.

I didn't think much of it at the time. I nodded my head and smiled, thinking it was a fun idea, but then I went about my day as usual. But then something lovely happened. People started commenting and emailing me, saying that the concept had lifted immense stress from their lives. The ladder analogy had permitted them to stop trying to be at the top all the time, especially when they were just getting started.

Like any good online business owner would do, I saw an opportunity, I got excited about it, and then proceeded to sit on it for six months. But the idea kept nagging at me, and I found that I kept mentioning it and using it, until one day I saw my copy of Big Magic by Elizabeth Gilbert and remembered what she said about ideas being alive. If I didn't nurture this idea, then it would leave me and find someone else to give it the love it deserved. Well, I didn't want my idea to leave me; I knew then that I wanted to give it the respect it deserved and help it come to life.

And that is how The Ladder Principle was born.

2

The Ladder Principle

Your business is like a ladder. When you decide to start any business, you have to make some critical decisions about what it will look like and how it will function. In this book, we are mainly talking about online businesses because that's where I live and what I know, but I believe the principle applies to all entrepreneurs.

You first have to pick your ladder, put it together and then begin to climb. Most of the time we come up with a brilliant idea, we give it a name, and then we tell everyone we are the CEO of that business. But are we really? The glaring truth is that we aren't even close to being the CEO of anything yet. We are more like the parent or babysitter of the idea until we can bring it to life and get it going, and then it's a long, usually bumpy road to accomplish everything that needs to be done to make the business work and succeed.

Everyone starts at the bottom of their own ladder. And you should start at the bottom with pride. You labored and built that ladder, and for goodness sake, that is an amazing first step! Imagine all of the people out there that have ideas swirling around in their heads, but for whatever reason, they never take the action needed to bring it into the world and proclaim that it is theirs. You are already amazing if you have an idea, decide to take action, and then find yourself looking up at a wonderful new business where you get to climb your ladder.

I know, I know, looking up to the unknown can be scary. It sounds like it would be way more fun to be at the top and look down, but actually, it's scarier. Why? Well, when you try to start at the top, you will find that a few crucial things are missing.

First, you don't have the experience to understand how to fill that role. Imagine going into work every day where you don't really how what you should do or how to do it because you never did the work before or received the education needed to make decisions in that particular role. It sounds pretty stressful because IT IS!.

Second, most of the time you won't believe you belong there. That is where terms like 'imposter syndrome' come up, and you feel like people will see you as a fake, or realize you have no idea what you're doing. These are legitimate fears because let's be honest, you don't know what you are doing yet. You may be an expert in your field, but you aren't an expert at running your business yet, so why try to pretend?

The Ladder Principle is all about understanding that there is a logical progression of roles you will play in your business as it grows. To succeed you need to embrace each role with excitement, know when it's time to move to the next step, find a person or a system to take over the position you are leaving, and begin fulfilling your future role.

This book is all about walking you through this process and showing you exactly how to climb your ladder. Use it as a guide, use it as a map, use it in whatever way works for you, but make sure you use it.

Now the disclaimer: I am going to beat you over the head with the ladder analogy, because I want to ingrain these concepts into your brain, not only so that it can help you make important decisions in your business, but also help you stop beating yourself up so much.

What do you say? Are you with me?

For this to work though, you have to be in 100%. This book is playful and serious all at the same time. It will give you guidance as well as space, but it won't do what it's meant to do if you are secretly trying to skip steps while you think no one is looking. Let's work through this together; it's always smart to have someone to hold your ladder steady anyway so let that person be me right now.

3

Everyone Starts at the Bottom

If you started your career in an intern position at any company, you would approach climbing the corporate ladder as everyone else does. You would pay your dues getting coffee while soaking up all the knowledge you can until the time comes to move to the next position. That entry-level position would take another year, and hopefully, you would continue to move up the ladder at a nice steady pace. Maybe you have a mentor that helps you set a twenty-year career path plan so you can get all excited about where your life is going. Oh yeah, you heard me right, a twenty-year plan. That's because most careers within an organization can take that long to get to the top, or anywhere close to the top. Don't forget that you are competing with everyone else that wants to get to the top too so that that ladder can get pretty crowded and competitive.

These days people jump corporate ladders every few years trying to get to the top faster, but the climb is still slow.

If you decide to start your own business, especially online, you might have thought you get to skip climbing the ladder altogether and go straight to the top. That might sound amazing, but that's not how it works. You might move faster and make more money than you thought possible, but you still have to make the climb.

When you start your own business, you start at the bottom. Embrace the fact that you will be doing the grunt work, getting the coffee, and soaking up all the knowledge of the people ahead of you. This is your time to take it all in, get your hands dirty, and make it happen. This step on the ladder and every other level is vital to your journey, and you should embrace it with excitement and dedication.

The challenge we face is trying to climb our ladder too fast. Clamoring to get to the top so that we can say that we are 'the boss,' only to feel the stress when we don't have all the systems, people, or personal training in place to embody the role.

Just because you started the business doesn't mean you are a CEO, it means you are the founder of something awesome, but you have to give yourself time to earn the right to call yourself the CEO, and it shouldn't be rushed.

Don't get me wrong; you might be able to get there a heck of a lot faster than if you were working for someone else, but don't beat yourself up when you are only six months into launching your business, and you aren't operating at CEO status. If you were an intern at a company and somehow moved up to CEO in six months they would make documentaries about you because let's be real; it just doesn't happen that fast, so why would it happen that way for your own business?

So cut yourself some slack.

You have permission to take it one step at a time. I am going to walk you through why taking it one step at a time is better for your business and you.

You can climb your ladder with less stress and more success if you follow the model I am about to lay out for you. This in no way means that everything in your business will go right, or that you will make tons of money. What I promise is not fame and fortune, although that might be in your future, and I hope that you get whatever you want in life. What I can offer you is a path that will help you make decisions in your business, cut down on the stress from trying to move too fast, and help you climb your ladder with grace so that when the time comes, you can seize that CEO role with sustainable success.

4

You Can Only Climb
One Ladder at a Time

We all have a ton of ideas swirling around in our heads at one time or another. I rarely find the kind of person that ends up starting a business sitting around struggling to think up ideas of what to start. The real problem is figuring out which idea you like the best, will have a good chance at being successful, and be something you can commit to seeing it through.

Here's a problem: we aren't always so great at committing to one thing. We think that multi-tasking is a strength, but when it comes to multiple business ideas, trying to bring two ideas to life at the same time is a lot like trying to climb two ladders at once. Yikes, and ouch! I love the ladder analogy because it helps you visualize one significant factor: risk.

"Risk" is defined as 'a situation involving exposure to danger' or 'to expose (someone or something valued) to danger, harm, or loss.' That sounds pretty serious, no wonder most of us naturally avoid risk. That sounds like it might hurt.

Even with risk looming out there, all those ideas in our heads want to be heard, so its no wonder so many online entrepreneurs end up starting multiple businesses. These great ideas seem like they really could work, so why not try them all, right? Well, let's think about your different business as ladders and see how that works.

You are working your way through different roles while building one business, say it's a website design business, and you are busy climbing that ladder. You get an idea and decide to start a T-shirt business because, after all, you know how to design. Now you have two ladders. To manage both companies, you need to be able to jump from one ladder to the next. You need to be ready to go back and forth.

Imagine you are half way up that website design ladder, and you need to jump over to the T-shirt business ladder. In this case, the business has the design element in common so let's say the ladders are pretty close to each other. You have both hands on one ladder, and you move one foot to the other ladder. You need to be steady and slow to make sure you don't fall off. You take your time and slowly move to the next ladder. Phew, you made it. That took time and was a bit scary.

Now imagine you are moving back and forth from one ladder to the next day after day. You need to get faster, so you stop taking so much precious time and all of a sudden your risk of falling goes up.

Of course, it is possible that you never fall, and both business ladders remain sturdy, and you can jump back and forth, but you know what doesn't happen so fast? You don't move up either ladder as fast as you could. You might not move up either ladder at all. You spend so much time focusing on moving between ladders that you can't focus on how to climb higher on either ladder.

The reason I enjoy the ladder analogy so much is because it gets us to think about the risk we are taking by trying to do too many things at once. You need to be able to focus on one ladder at a time to stay steady and grow. If you want to claim that CEO status at the top of your ladder, then you need to focus on only one ladder at a time.

I'm not saying you can't climb more than one ladder in your lifetime. I'm saying you shouldn't climb more than one ladder at a time. As we talk through the different roles you will need to take on at each step of your business ladder you will begin to see why having focus is so important and when it might be time to start a new ladder.

But for now, let's commit to only climbing one ladder at a time.

5

You Need a Stable Ladder

Have you ever owned a real ladder? They all come with a huge bright colored sign right on the side that says someone should always hold the ladder while you climb. That means climbing a real ladder is something you shouldn't do alone and it turns out climbing your business ladder is no different.

I see it over and over and over and over again. Was that too many 'overs'? Well, I see it a lot. People everywhere are starting businesses online and then trying to do everything in their business by themselves, they don't find a community to talk to when things go wrong, and they wear their 'busy' like a badge of pride. I did it when I started my first online business adventure, and it didn't work then, and guess what? It doesn't work now.

There are three things you need to make sure you have the right support for your business ladder. 1. A community of like-minded people who understand what you are trying to achieve and want to cheer you on and support you. 2. A smaller group of people at about the same level as you in your businesses to bounce ideas off each other and help you make decisions. We call this a mastermind. 3. A coach or mentor who is farther up their ladder than you are who you can look up to for advice and wisdom. All three of these are required to make sure you have a steady ladder.

The thing that people don't realize is that you can't ask the same person or group to hold your ladder all the time, that would be exhausting for them. Instead, having all three kinds of support allow you to lean on different support systems at different times. Now you have rotating support, and you can confidently begin climbing your ladder because you know someone is always holding it steady for you.

When you know that you are being supported in the right way, you feel better about moving your business forward. You will probably feel more excited, connected, and motivated to do the hard work needed to get to the top.

If you aren't sure how to find people that 'get you' don't worry, I have a free training on how to engage in online communities and find your tribe. Just go to www.boss-mom.com/tribe, and it will walk you through a two-week process to find your people. Once you find your tribe, the right people to be in a small thinktank mastermind with you will reveal itself. Having a mastermind to help you talk through decisions in your business is so important to helping you climb your ladder.

Once you have a tribe, most likely people will recommend the right mentor for you, so finding the right online tribe is the perfect first step.

6

How I Picked My Ladder

I grew up in a pretty creative and entrepreneurial family, but I still looked at the world very logically. I knew I needed to go to college, which I did, and I knew I needed to get a job, which I did. I pretty much wandered from small business to small business trying to figure out what I wanted to do and who I wanted to be. I would pick up some excellent skills and love parts of each job, and then get bored or unhappy within a year. If this sounds familiar, you see that you are not alone.

Even my college major was pretty random. Someone recently asked me if I was a passionate writer or if I was involved with my high school newspaper because my major was journalism, and the answer is… not even close. My step-dad rented Up Close and Personal for me to watch one night. It's about Michelle Pfeiffer trying to make it in the broadcast world, and she falls in love with Robert Redford. It was a beautiful movie, and after I watched it, I immediately thought I wanted to be a news anchor. My step-dad, my first mentor, totally knew what he was doing. So I got a degree in broadcast journalism because I watched a romantic drama and thought it looked cool. I now realize my step-dad saw some skill in me that I didn't see at the time and knew how to guide me in the right direction. I am forever grateful because I believe my degree is pretty much the single best learning experience I could have gotten to prepare me for owning an online business.

Fast forward seven years from college, and you would find me sitting in the basement of my CEO's house along with 30 other employees from all different levels of the organization to go through a facilitated experience where we helped decide the future of the company's culture as it grew. It was fascinating to watch, and it was there that I was introduced to the first mentor that would put the bug in my ear to step out on my own.

He selected a few other participants and me to be co-facilitators. I didn't even know what that was at the time, and if you know me, you know I like to talk, so helping guide people instead of give people answers was a very foreign and uncomfortable thing for me. It was also one of the most amazing experiences of my life. And after the multi-day experience was over, this new mentor took me aside and said I had potential and that I should explore the possibility of starting my own consulting business.

It sounded exciting and terrifying, and I had no intention of actually doing it anytime soon. I was going to think about it, wish for it, and then pretty much not act on it. Instead, I decided to try to write a book about how to advance your career. Come to think of it; the book would have been just like Climb

Your Own Ladder, except for a corporate setting. Ha, go figure.

Not long after that, the business I worked for was making a shift, and I could see that my position would no longer be mine, so I proactively told them I would resign in 90 days to give me time to prepare my team and to find something new. It seemed scary and a bit sad at the time, but it was the best kick in the butt I could have ever gotten. Sometimes we need people to push us out into the open to force us to do what we should do, but don't dare to do.

After the 90 days and a ton of conversations with my mentor and my husband, I decided to try that whole own your own consulting business thing for a while. We decided we would give it three months to see how it went and then decide if I would continue on my own or get a new job. Be careful if you take this path because once you have a taste of creating your own thing, it's tough to imagine ever going back to working for someone else.

After six weeks of trying to figure out my brand, website, logo, packages and all that fun stuff, I found out I was pregnant. It turns out when everyone takes you out for tequila on your last night of a job it can end with having babies. I like to say that I became an entrepreneur and a mom on the same day. My husband used to say that was too much information, but I suppose if you can't handle the idea of where babies come from, then you aren't going to be able to stomach all the crazy parts of owning a business.

A lot of people don't know this, but Boss Mom was not the first business ladder I created. Boss Mom is the only ladder I built and climbed, but I spent two years trying to climb a completely different ladder and to be honest I never really got past the first step.

I had a fascination with behavioral psychology, behavioral economics, and mindful communication. I spent a lot of time at my previous job taking classes and studying how people communicate and connect. I was in a director position for the first time, and I wanted to be a leader, but I had no idea how. I quickly realized that everyone communicates differently, feels valued differently, and reacts differently. I wanted to understand people so that I could lead them better.

When I started my own business, it seemed logical to do mindful communication training. Yep, that's the first ladder I picked. I got a few jobs doing leadership and communication training for various companies and spent most of my first pregnancy trying to decide on a business name, logo, and website design. Looking back those were not the right places to spend my time, but I didn't know that back then. It was an uphill battle, and while I do love mindful communication and believe it is key to good leadership and thriving relationships, it's not my gift and the business never really made any money. If I think about it, it never really got to be a business, it was more like an idea that didn't work. Looking back, I'm not sure I even figured out what my ladder looked like so no wonder I never got to the climbing stage.

The defining moment when I decided to pick a different ladder happened at a conference in Irvine, California. I went with my best friend because she had a free ticket. We were both skeptical of the event and didn't expect much. We walked in and sat down, and both decided it wasn't the right fit for us, but that we would stay until lunch. I don't specifically remember any of the speakers, but I do remember one gentleman who had been in the military who got up on stage and said something that would change my life forever. He said, "as entrepreneurs, we feel like we are pretty good at a lot of things, but when you find that one thing that takes you less time than it takes everyone else to do, then you have something you can sell and scale." Well, I think that's what he said, at least that's what I heard.

That statement hit me hard. The whole mindful communication thing wasn't coming easily to me at all. Everything I did felt hard. My friend and I left the conference and decided to hunker down at a coffee shop the whole next day and work on our businesses, but I didn't know what I was going to do or change so I told her we should work together on her stuff.

Several hours in she looked up at me and said, "Dana, this is what you should be doing." I had no idea what she was talking about, so she explained it: over the last few hours I had helped her see how the pieces of her business puzzle fit together, what content she should create, and how her programs should be structured.

Duh, of course. Back in several of my corporate jobs, I had been in charge of building coursework and content for our clients, and I had a degree that gave me skills in writing, video, and design. Why on earth had I not seen it before? The answer is that we rarely see the things that are right in front of us. That's why we need that support system I was talking about earlier. They help us open our eyes and have mind-blowing ah-ha moments.

So I went home and went to the online community I was hanging out in at the time, and asked if anyone wanted to create a course, that I would coach them for free, and I was willing to take on three people. Within an hour ten people responded. I was off to the races. That is how the Expand Your Reach ladder was born. I made a quick logo and started to dive into building content for people and to test out what people would pay for and how my business would work. I was in the intern step (we will talk about that later) where I mainly learned a lot but didn't get paid much. I was doing what came naturally to me, and I was good at it, but it still felt hard.

About six months later I was given a free ticket to an event called the Best Year Ever Blueprint that was put on by a man named Hal Elrod. I would then find out he had written this insanely successful book called the Miracle Morning and was a beautiful and brilliant person. At that event, I connected with new people and was invited to be a part of a small think tank mastermind so that we could help each other grow our businesses.

One of my mastermind members was a book coach, and he offered to give me a great deal on coaching if I wanted to write a book. I had always wanted to say I was an author and believed it would establish me as an authority and help my business, so I said yes. My family and friends had mixed feelings about whether writing a book was a good idea. They felt like it would take away from my focus on my business, but as I was looking at my business ladder it seemed really out of focus, and I had no idea how to get to the next step.

I started the journey of writing the book that would become Boss Mom and would bring my ladder into focus and launch something life-changing.

I didn't realize it at the time, but I had been stuck looking up at my ladder and spinning my wheels trying to figure out how to make more money and get my business to grow when the fact was I didn't know why I was building the ladder in the first place.

I needed the movement and the purpose to help bring my ladder into focus and give me the clarity to know how I wanted my ladder to look, and how far I wanted to climb. Even now I am not quite there yet, and that's ok. I would say I am more like an Executive Vice President (EVP) in my own business, but I am steadily climbing my ladder, and I couldn't be happier.

PART 2

Creating
Your Ladder

I admire the courage and self-reliance it takes to start your own business and make it succeed.

Martha Stewart

7

Building the Sides of Your Ladder

Not everyone wants the same things. Some people want to be on the cover of magazines, own mansions, or be able to travel around the world all year long. Other people have a yearning to be creative in the world and make a good living doing what they love. And others want to do something they enjoy for vacation money. Our goals and aspirations all look different, and by the way, that's a good thing. The key is to understand what you want to build and what you want to achieve.

All ladders have two sides and steps, they aren't that complicated, and your business shouldn't be either. Trying to make your business super complicated will only make it harder to make decisions and take action, and for most of us, a complicated business isn't a requirement to be successful.

To feel confident about climbing your ladder you need stability. If you don't feel safe climbing your ladder, or your ladder feels out of focus, like mine did, then you'll be leery of climbing up. Remember, the sides of your ladder create stability. They are what hold your ladder together, and the analogy works perfectly for your business because there are a few core elements you need to have in your business to make sure it all holds together.

First, you need to decide what problem you want to solve. You are starting, or have started, a business because you want to solve a problem. It might be a problem you ran into and decided to create a solution for yourself and then discovered the rest of the world needed it too. I often hear women in the Boss Mom community saying that they don't solve a problem, they make a product or provide a service. The fact is we all solve a problem. That problem might be that people don't have the skill needed to execute that website design so they need to have someone who can bring their vision to life. Or maybe it's time to take newborn pictures, and they want to make sure everyone knows they are a girl and your custom pink hair bows are just the solution. If you don't know what problem you solve, then it's an uphill battle to get people to see why they need you, and you will continuously waver on what packages or products you will offer because you don't have a clear vision of what you are doing for your clients. This can make for a very wobbly ladder, and that's not what you want.

Second, you need to know how you will make money. There are a ton of people that say they want to put something out into the world and they will think about how they will monetize later. I am all for doing certain things for free in your business in the beginning as a rite of passage (we will talk about that in the Intern section), but you need to think through how you CAN make money in your business. You don't have to have all the answers at this point, but you need to have some idea of how you will make money in your business or else you will spend a lot of time at the bottom of your ladder, and that can get very lonely and exhausting.

I thought about whether knowing your purpose needed to be one of the foundations of your ladder, but the more I thought about it and as I interviewed women on the Boss Mom Podcast, it became clear that purpose is something that is revealed to us as we climb our ladder. If we wait to try to start climbing our ladder until we understand our exact purpose, then we may never begin to the climb because we usually gain clarity during the climb. It's good to think about why you decided to start your business, but don't get hung up on the real purpose and essence of why you wake up in the morning and do what you do. The answer will reveal itself to you along the way.

Now that we have the sides of our ladder, we need to decide how tall you want your ladder to be. Knowing how high you want your ladder to go is important because it helps you see how far you need to go, and how far you have climbed. If your ladder seems to have no end, then you will end up burnt out and exhausted, and I don't want that for you.

So how do you decide how tall your ladder should be? Well, here are a few things you need to decide to build your business ladder.

Question 1: What is your ideal business size? Do you want to be a consultant with no full-time employees? Do you want to have a physical office with a whole gaggle of people? Or maybe it's somewhere in between. Think about what you are about to create. You might not have all of the answers, but don't skip this part of the process. Thinking about it now will help keep it fresh in your mind as you begin to build and grow your business. As situations come up that give you more insight into what you want, you will be more open to seeing the teaching lesson and applying it to how you are structuring your business. For instance, you decide in the beginning that you want to keep your business small with just you so that it's always flexible and easy. But as you begin to hit your capacity of clients, you realize you do want to bring on a team member to help you create space for more clients. Or on the other side, you decide you want to create a huge world-dominating business, but as you build up a book of clients, you realize that you want more space and time to grow your family and that means growing slower. Both of these are ok realizations to have. Pretty much every entrepreneur makes these internal pivots in their business from time to time.

Question 2: How much time do you want to spend in your business each week? Is this business full-time or something you will do on the side? It is a good idea to think about what your minimum and maximum hours are for each week. This means that if something takes you away from work, like a sick child, what is the minimum effort you can put into your business to keep it running. And if a project needs to get done, how much extra time are you able to put in to get it done? These are such important questions because they can help you create a business that gives you energy instead of draining your energy.

I remember when I launched Boss Mom I wanted to take over the world. I still do, but after being in business for several years, I want to grow my business in a different way. I didn't mind the idea of working a full week in the beginning. I was willing to do whatever it took to get the business off the ground. That meant working a lot of nights after the kids went to bed. After a while, I realized I hadn't read a book that wasn't a business book in a long time. I was always the last one up, and my business was mostly all I ever thought about each day. I decided that I was only willing to work three nights a week and that meant I needed to change how I was running my business and spending my time. A year after that I decided I was willing to keep my revenue the same and work on cutting my hours in half. The point is that my time priorities changed as I grew my business and that's ok. You might decide to work more as you grow your business and that's ok too. Do what feels right and works for you. Make a decision now about how much time you want to spend in your business and then see how it feels. Start with an idea in mind and then tweak from there.

8

How To Decorate Your Ladder

If you thought your ladder was only visible to you, then you couldn't be more wrong. In today's online and visible day and age, your brand and business are more out in the world than ever before. If you build the right ladder and climb it the right way, then you will be excited and proud to show it off to the world, even when things don't go exactly as you planned.

Decorating your ladder is a lot like decorating your room. It is an expression of your personality, what you care about, and what you are trying to accomplish or change in the world. Your ladder brand should exude the parts of your character and flair that will resonate and attract your perfect tribe, but for now, let's focus on the parts of you that you want to splash up on that ladder; kind of like stickers on your car.

To start, think about the personality traits that you want the world to see and resonate with immediately. Is your ladder going to be playful and colorful, or maybe elegant with a lot of white space. What kinds of quotes or sayings would you be willing to stick to your ladder for all to see? Your brand is incredibly important to attracting the right people to your team and business. We could fill a whole book about the importance of branding, but for now, let's say that deciding how you want your ladder to be seen by others is an important concept to think through as you build your ladder.

9

Not all ladders are the same

Each of us is unique characters building beautiful things in the world, so it makes sense that we will all build unique businesses. That said, if you want to start, grow, and scale a business there is a framework that you can use to make your life a lot easier and the path a lot less painful.

I believe that you need to feel the pains of failure, and lucky for us both there is pretty much no way around it when you build a business. Some things are going to work, and some things aren't.

You might try to emulate a business you admire only to see that what worked for them crashes and burns for you. That is just the way the world works. You should still try to find people you respect, and books you can read that will give you ideas and advice on what to do in your business. It is far better to listen to those who have climbed their ladder, and of course, learn from their mistakes, than to close yourself off and try to do everything yourself.

Yes, you are unique, and your path to climbing your ladder is one that only you can experience, but let those supporting you be there to keep you steady and help you decide when to take that next step. And while on your journey of discovery for your business, recognize that what you end up with will be a unique recipe made up of all of the tools and tactics that you learned, and that in the end, it will morph from other people's methods to your unique process and success. Always remember those who helped you get there, but at the same time, own that you are the one that ultimately made it happen.

10

You can't skip steps

When we started on this whole journey together (reading this book of course) you promised to commit to climbing your ladder and not skipping steps. The challenge is that everyone wants to skip steps; it's human nature, we can't help ourselves. I remember practicing piano and wishing that I could be able to play the song without all the work or reading a business book wishing I just knew the information without having to read it, so I could start implementing right away.

I won't be the first one to tell you that the pain, the joy, and the success is in the journey, but I am going to attempt to frame it a different way for you here so that maybe it will sink in and stick.

When we talk about enjoying the journey it all seems vague, doesn't it? It's not clear when the journey starts, where it ends, when the pain will strike, and when the lessons will be learned. With all those unknowns it's no wonder that people don't embrace the whole 'success is in the journey' concept.

So let's make that journey a whole lot clearer by showing you a vivid picture of a ladder and the steps involved. Once we walk you through the steps, you will see how you will climb your ladder, the steps involved, the natural places you will feel climbing pains, and all the fun in-between.

So why is the journey the critical part anyway? That's a great question.

I believe that there are a few aspects of really going through an experience that changes the way we see the world. Before we experience something, we don't believe we can do it; we doubt ourselves. Before we experience something, we can't confidently explain all steps of the process, and we don't understand the nuances of the process so we can't create systems and automation.

Taking in every aspect of our journey has benefits that far surpass the negative components, and you can't avoid experiencing your journey, so it's pointless to try. The only terrible thing you can do is to fight or skip the process. When you try to skip the journey or in other words, climbing your ladder, you end up blocking your ability to take in all the possible lessons and strategy that comes out of your experience. You are, in effect, sabotaging your ability to succeed.

As we walk through each step you need to climb while growing your business, you might think to yourself that the role doesn't sound all that wonderful, but there is no escaping the fact that you cannot skip steps. Every business owner will tell you it's a rite of passage to climb your ladder. So really, ignoring this fact will cause more stress, guilt, and waste precious time you could be using to learn valuable lessons and move forward quicker.

The bottom line, embrace each step, learn all you can, read my methodology and learn when to move up in your ladder, and enjoy the pain and the success that comes with owning your own business.

PART 3

The Steps
on Your Ladder

Good ideas are common,
but those who are
willing to take action and
execute those ideas
are far more rare.

Pat Flynn

11

How a ladder works

Now that you have your ladder built it's time to start the climb. Before you can get started you need to understand one crucial factor; you will not be the only one on your ladder. Each step on your ladder represents a role you must play in your business. Once you are ready to make a move up, you will need to replace yourself with a system or a person. Each role and step that we talk about will walk you through the position in your business, what it includes, why you need to be there, how to know when it's time to move up, how to replace yourself in that role, and how to get to the next step quicker.

No matter where you think you are on your ladder right now, I recommend you read through each step anyway. This book is a quick and fun read, and a little reflection is always good to make sure you are doing what is best for your business and you. Now, let's have a little fun, shall we?

12

The Intern

I know that your business was your idea. And I know that you technically own the company, but there is just no way to avoid the intern phase. Don't worry; this can be a fun phase of learning and growth. You should approach it just like an internship.

So what is the function of an internship and how do you know if you are on that step right now? An internship is all about learning and deciding your path. You get an internship to learn how to fill a particular role in a business, receive mentorship, and get an inside look at how a business actually works so you can decide if that business path is one you want to take. Being the intern is the perfect first role in your own business.

Your internship at your own business doesn't have to be long, but you should stay in the intern position until you have learned what you need to move up. Your internship may be paid or unpaid, but if you are getting paid that means the clients you are taking on at this rate are at a discount or beta rate and that's ok.

One of the first rules of being an intern is that it does not mean that you are inferior or less than anyone else or that you are not cut out to be the CEO of your own business. Starting in the intern position is merely a necessary step you need to take to get to know your business better and soak up knowledge so that you can move up with confidence.

Take this time to be humble.

Even if you have a degree or experience in your particular field, you probably didn't go to business school and also if you did, owning your own business is a whole new beast so don't walk in thinking you know everything. Take advice when given and let it soak in to get a sense of what feels right to you. Ask a lot of questions and come to the intern position with enthusiasm and excitement.

Not sure who to take advice from or where to ask questions? Offer up services to your ideal client, even if it's for free, and then ask them to give you feedback on what worked and what didn't. Ask your community what they want to see. Connect with influencers in your space and ask to pick their brain or buy their programs. This is a time of hard work and learning. At this stage, you will not receive a lot of money, but you will gain clarity and knowledge and those are incredibly valuable assets to have as you climb your ladder.

Two of the winning attributes of an intern are initiative and adaptability. Embody these two traits if you want to rock your intern role and move to the next position quickly.

Adaptability is all about rolling with the punches and making changes where needed. You may be trying to hone in on your brand at this time in your business or beginning to offer up services to your target audience. The more you listen and observe in this phase the better because you will need to see what works and what doesn't and adapt. Take the initiative and try new things. Don't put all of your efforts into one large idea that will take forever to execute and no one will see for months. Instead, listen to your audience and create what makes sense and test it out. The quicker you do this, the faster you will be able to gain clarity on your sweet spot and move into higher paying roles with less work and more clout.

You will be thankful you put the work into the intern phase and will appreciate what it took to move you to the next step on your ladder.

When you notice that you don't have to look for so many answers and can complete projects quicker that is a good sign that you are about to move up the ladder. You will begin to get more clients and feel less inclined to offer up services or programs at a deep discount. In most cases, you will naturally move up to the next roll and won't notice until you are right in the thick of a lot of fires and clean up.

Who will take over your role in this step? The great thing about the intern position is that no one will take over for you, you just move up. This is pretty much the only role where there is no real automation or a person that will take over. Congratulations, you are now ready to be the Janitor.

13

The Janitor

I wish I could tell you that the next step in your ladder was a little more glamorous, but the role that now needs to be filled right now is the janitor role. That's right; you get to clean up a lot of messes and put out a lot of fires at this stage of your business and growth.

Don't worry, this is a super important role, and you should be proud to be here; it means you have created a legit online business. If nothing were going on, then there would be nothing to fix. Take it as a good sign. The janitor is all about creating space and setting things so that you can make your business exponentially better.

If you don't recognize you are in this role and embrace it the right way, you may find yourself in a perpetual cycle of cleaning up urgent but not important messes, and that's not a good place to get stuck. So let's get you acclimated to this role so that you can own it and then move on quickly.

There are two aspects to the janitor role. There are the routine inspections and maintenances that are needed to run your business, and then there are the reactive cleanups that will inevitably be required. If you rocked the intern step, then you have all the knowledge you need to move through this role. I know what you are thinking, and no, you don't know everything you need to know to be the CEO….but you do know everything and more that you need to know to tackle the janitor role like a Rockstar.

Now, you might be asking yourself, "How do I ever get out of the janitor role? Aren't we always cleaning up messes in our businesses?" The answer is, to some degree, yes, however, the goal in the janitor role is to do five things.

1. Identify one-off issues versus repeated issues

2. Create a process for people to handle all kinds of problems in the future systematically

3. Figure out which issues could be fixed with a better system or process

4. Figure out which issues arise because you are not working with your ideal client

5. Create a plan to enhance your processes and systems to lower the number of issues.

When it comes to cleaning up, automation and delegation can take a great amount of stress off of you, and the janitor role.

The key to moving through the janitor role is not simply to resolve issues. The key is to learn from the issues that arise and make the needed shifts in the way you run your business and what you offer. If you start with the one or two offerings that you're great at and continuing to refine those skills, then you will be able to move out of the janitor role quicker. If you find yourself stuck in the janitor role, it may be that you're trying to do too many new things all at once and not giving yourself the chance to refine your systems.

If you are feeling stuck in the janitor phase of your business don't worry, you can break the cycle. Here are a few situations to help you know if you are stuck in the janitor role.

1. You want to delegate some of your day-to-day administrative work, but you don't have the systems in place to be able to hand anything off to anyone other than yourself.

2. All of your knowledge is in your head, which means you are the only one that can do anything.

3. You keep having to repeat yourself or a process when it comes to customer service because you don't have a process in place that allows your customer to troubleshoot for themselves.

These are all prevalent challenges that come up in a growing business, but how long we choose to let them persist is up to us.

You can either keep things as they are and wake up with same issues that only you can solve, or you can decide you want to keep moving up your ladder and automate or delegate these issues one-by-one until you have enough extra free time to move to the next step.

14

The Internal Service Provider

Welcome to your new role as your very own internal service provider. Guess what? That means you get to learn new tools and how to build stuff. Are you an expert in any of these fields? Probably not. Will you ever be an expert in any of these fields? Probably not. Unless one of these is your area of expertise, like building websites or writing copy, then odds are, you're just gonna have to learn it for now until you can afford to have somebody else that's better than you do it for you. Don't worry; you are not alone. Unless you started with a ton of money, you're going to need to be your internal service provider for a while.

In most situations, I think it's smart to experience each step on your ladder for yourself, but there are some areas where you might not have the technical skills to execute what you want to do for your business. For instance, do you have to build your website to be successful? No. I would say that if you can have somebody else create your website in the beginning and save yourself the time, then that's great. Here's the thing though. You don't want to buy yourself a high-end website in the beginning, because I can pretty much guarantee that within a year you will be changing at least some element of your brand and have a burning desire to redo the whole site. Keep your costs low in the beginning, even if you have the cash.

Same goes for learning social media tools and understanding how they work. I hope that during your intern phase you did a lot of learning, so you have some idea of some of the images and content that needs to be created to build an audience. This might mean that you're writing your social media content, building your own website, writing your mass emails, making your sales funnel, creating your own opt-in, writing your sales pages, doing your sales calls, doing your own follow up, and pretty much anything else that needs to be created or done. That also means that you are doing all of the administrative tasks as well, like scheduling your flights, reviewing your emails, and the list goes on.

It's a busy time in your business. It's busy because hopefully, you're starting to get a more steady stream of clients. During this phase, you will feel a little bit overwhelmed. It's hard to be your service provider, and be the salesperson, and also do client work.

In the end, this phase can last a long time, or it can be short, depending on your budget, what you get good at and how much you are willing to pay. If you can invest in a business coach at this point in your career, it's not a bad idea. Join a group coaching program. Get a one-on-one coach. Buy a course that will teach you some of the elements that you need to learn to move forward. If you want to have a short call with me to figure out the next step in your business go to www.boss-mom.com/fitting and we can have a quick chat.

15

The Closer

In the beginning, you probably leveraged existing relationships to get clients. You had a few wins, got a few referrals and it seemed like you were on a roll, and then things started to slow down. All of a sudden you have to figure out how to bring in new traffic to your website and social media and turn cold leads into new clients. You have become your own sales rep or 'the closer.' The land of sales can be a scary place for many new online entrepreneurs, but no matter how much you wish you didn't have to "sell" you need to get comfy with the idea that if you want to run your own online business, then you have to learn how to sell.

Sales mode is a crucial step in your ladder, and I recommend that you embrace this role no matter how uncomfortable or terrible it feels. Later in your business, you never know when you might lose a sales rep or end up in a situation where you need to ensure you are bringing in revenue and you should be able to pitch your product or service and close the sale confidently. Very few people are great at selling right out of the gate so embrace the pain, and you will continually get better and sell more.

Now, being a sales rep in your own business means you have to create a business habit like a salesperson would where you are consistently reaching out, always following up, and continuously asking for the sale. I remember somebody recently asking me how I could get people to give them more money, and I asked her how many times that week they'd asked somebody to give them money. They said zero. I said, "Well, how do you expect anybody to give you money if you're not asking for it?" And it was one of those moments where they went, "That's a good point. How do I get in more situations where I can ask people for money?" I said, "Well, now you're starting to think like a salesperson. Where are these people hanging out? How can you hang out in that place more? What are the questions we need to ask to understand if they are a good fit and if they are the ideal person that would potentially get value from your program."

The closer role is not necessarily fun, and it's not necessarily easy, and I will tell you that sometimes you are going to avoid it like the plague because when you sell some people will say to you 'no,' and that can sting. But if you do not embrace the 'no's' so that you can get to the 'yes's' then you are going to have a hard time growing your business and getting up to the next step in your ladder.

The bottom line is that it's your business, so it's your responsibility to ensure that you make sales, no one else will care about keeping your business alive more than you. At some point, you might hire someone else to be responsible for your sales, but in the beginning, it's just you. You're the one that has to continually convince people that what you have is valuable enough to pay you.

To get good at making sales, you need to practice. Unlike some of the other positions, you have experienced so far this position is all about repetition. I want you to get good at saying the same thing to new people instead of different things to the same people. It's not just about growing a small following. It's about becoming known, becoming the expert, and building clout in one particular area. That means as the closer you need to know what it is you're selling, what it looks like, why it's packaged that way, what you're going to deliver, and what problem it is going to solve. The clearer you can get on this, the better, and repetition is your path to clarity and confidence.

In addition to being utterly confident in what problem you solve and what you sell, you will need to have absolute clarity in your ideal clients...

1. Frustrations
2. What perfect future they want
3. How they think and act
4. What you have in common
5. What their world looks like if they don't take action
6. What motivates them to action

Once you know these things, then getting clients is as simple as following these eight steps.

1. Connect with people online or in person
2. Get people on your email list so that you can continually talk to them
3. Talk with those people often
4. Tell them about your product or service
5. Ask them to buy your product or service
6. Handle any objections that would keep them from buying your product or service
7. Understand your conversion rates so that you can continually get better

8. Repeat one through seven until you take over the world

Now, I know that sounds simple, and that's because it is simple.

To create sales for your business, you need to reach out repetitively. You need to talk to people proactively. You need to get those people into your email list so that you can talk to them more than once. You need to tell those same people about what it is you do and what you sell. Then you need to ask those people to buy your stuff. And when they say 'no' or don't respond, you need to keep in touch and find ways to keep asking until you confirm they aren't a good fit or they convert into a client.

You would be amazed at how many people don't follow this process. I was one of those people for a long time. I was active on social media and talked to people all the time, but rarely was I systematically reaching out to highly targeted prospects and working to make a sale. I was hoping that it would happen in a more organic, authentic way, but the fact is that closers have focus and they know what their end goal is, and you need to find that focus if you want to make consistent sales in your business.

You need to remember that being the closer isn't just about convincing other people that we are worth spending their money. It's about convincing ourselves that our business is worth all of the effort, all of the pain that it takes to make it work and to make it thrive. When you consistently make this sales process a part of your weekly habit, then you are showing yourself, and the world that you are serious about your business and you intend to make it a success.

Once you are generating consistent revenue, you can decide if the sales role is one you want to outsource. Certain people are built for sales and find a deep sense of satisfaction in asking for the sale. If this isn't you, and you would prefer to focus on your area of expertise that is now growing in demand because of all of your hard work, then invest in a sales rep that can take calls for you. If most of your sales are from webinars, live training, or email, then it might be time to bring in a sales funnel specialist to help you figure out how to scale your expertise.

The next position is all about being able to manage more of your operations on a higher, more complex level, so you're going to need a little extra mental space. I wish you luck. Being the closer in your own business can be scary and intimidating, but I promise that if you put in the effort, repeat often, and continually reach out and follow up, you will dominate this role and your business will thrive.

16

Project Manager/Operations Director

When I started writing this book, I kept going back and forth on whether the project manager role should go before the Internal Service Provider or Closer Role. In some ways, all of these positions overlap at some point or another, but after much reflection, I made a decision and placed the project manager role here.

Up until now, you have had projects and maybe even launches that needed to be managed. You might have also created project plans with due dates to help you stay on track and reach your goals.

The reason the project management role goes after the Closer position is that up until this point you are the primary team member in your business and your primary goal is to make revenue so that you can grow into a sustainable business. It is likely that up until now you haven't been able to create a long-term strategic plan for your business because you were so busy working in the day-to-day aspects of your business that there wasn't much time left for anything else.

Now that you have gotten your basic business systems in place and created recurring revenue for yourself, you have some space to start long-term planning. It's officially time to put on your project management hat.

The definition of project management is "the practice of initiating, planning, executing, controlling, and closing the work of a team to achieve specific goals and meet specific success criteria at the specified time. The primary challenge of project management is to achieve all of the project goals within the given constraints."

I think the end of that definition is so right. Finishing projects exactly how we envision them by the initial due date is sometimes virtually impossible. In the early stages of your business, so many things change that it's hard to have clear goals and deadlines. You aren't sure how long tasks will take, and sometimes we change our minds mid-project and end up pivoting altogether. But not anymore, right? You are ready to get focused and start planning strategically.

To implement strategic planning for your business, you have to know precisely how you're setting goals and building your team.

It's official, scaling your business has now become possible. Before, you would always hit that proverbial ceiling and run out of time or resources. There's a finite number of hours you or your team have to spend on particular items, and there's a limited amount of financial resources you have to put into your business. At the point where you're making consistent revenue, and you have systems in place, enough to allow you to predictably know how much money you will make depending on how much money you put into your business, you are now ready to embody the project management position and start to scale your business. That means that you know for a fact that if you put a dollar into your business, that it will yield, say, $2 or something like that. The main idea is that scalable is at least somewhat predictable to the amount you put in, to the amount that will come out. That means you have to have systems and trends.

Now, the reason you don't get to jump up to the CEO role just yet is that additional planning needs to happen. That means growing pains are about to hit. Yes, I'm sorry, you're about to have some growing pains. That's because all the systems that you used, in the beginning, to help you get clients as a solopreneur are not all going to continue to convert the same as you continue to grow as an organization.

I wish I could tell you that as your company gets bigger, that everything gets easier but that is not usually how it works.

Your business grows a lot like a child just when they master anew skill, BAM, they start to grow and need to learn a whole new set of skills.

As your business grows it changes, and there are going to be growing pains. This means that extra planning is so incredibly crucial.

Planning isn't always easy. This is one of those positions in your organization where it might be necessary to have someone outside of your organization, with a fresh perspective, to help pull everything that you want to accomplish out of your brain and put it into an actionable.

That's why this chapter is called Project Manager AND Operations Director, because it's not just about putting projects in place and making sure you hit deadlines. This position in your organization is also about creating a well-organized business, a focused business, a business that knows why it's doing what it's doing every single day and what those actions will give you back in return as you move forward.

This position is about setting yourself up to be able to scale in a way that doesn't drive you insane or burn you out. Nailing down your projects and operations and ensuring they are leading you in the right direction gives you room to move up into the CEO and Visionary position.

Now you are ready to relinquish some of the day-to-day tasks to someone else or an automated process so that you can become the CEO of your own business.

17

CEO & Visionary

So you made it to the top. Congratulations, you have built what we all hope is a successful, and hopefully sustainable business. You should give yourself a big hug because according to the Bureau of Labor Statistics, only about 50% of small businesses make it past four years, and 20% never make it past year one. That means you are part of an elite crowd and I think you are pretty awesome.

Being the CEO of your own business is a big responsibility and should not be taken lightly. It takes a lot of blood, sweat and tears to get to this point. It may feel like it was always your job to make the decisions about the future of your organization, but now that you have built a bona-fide successful business there is a lot more at stake.

So what exactly does the CEO position entail?

When I was growing up, we used to call my step-dad a "Go West" person. He would envision the future and boldly claim that we were going to achieve some seemingly impossible goal. We would all laugh and say, "Yeah, right." And then he would go off, and somehow, make it a reality.

The reason we called him a "Go West" person was not just because he was the visionary, but because he would forget simple daily items that came up in life and business. We would look at him and say, "Wow! You're so forgetful" or "Didn't you think of that detail?" But instead of looking at us embarrassed he would say, "That's not my job to remember those things. It is my job to envision the future and to never take my eyes off of that future. It is everybody else's job in my organization to make sure that we have everything in place to get where we want to go, to make sure we have the wagons and the beans and the sleeping bags so that we can actually go west."

He said, "It is my job to be focused on our future so intently, that when everybody's morale falters, and they begin to wonder whether or not our goals are possible, I can pull everybody back into focus with me. Every moment that I take my eyes off of that future, I risk us not getting there."

My step-father was my first mentor, and he didn't just make me want to be an entrepreneur, he made me want to be a leader.

I always wondered when I would be able to become a "Go West" person and I would like to think I am almost there.

If you want to know whether you are at the "Go West" level you only need to ask yourself two questions.

1. Can you set your sights on a goal, and believe in it so firmly that no one will be able to convince you that it's not possible.

2. Does your executive, or virtual assistant, look at you like you're an idiot sometimes wondering how you can be so smart and yet you seem to miss the most straightforward administrative details?

That second one isn't a joke. When you reach "Go West" status, I believe your brain does not have the space to worry about the smaller details like booking your travel plans for that business trip or remembering to print that agenda for a meeting.

Of course, you are capable of handling these details, and back in your intern phase you were probably really good at managing these tasks, but now your brain needs to focus on blazing a path, and that generally takes all of your brainpower.

Make sure you have someone on your team to manage those details. If you are at the CEO level, then you should have an executive assistant. If you don't have one, get one.

Be prepared because being the visionary of an organization is a stressful job. Those moments where you want to cry or give up... you can't. You are the rock that your team looks to for assurance that it's all going to be ok. Even though it's tough, sometimes you have to remain steadfast in your belief that what you're doing is the right thing to do. It may be hard to do, but it is one of the most important jobs of a CEO, and it is, in my opinion, what can make or break a growing and scaling organization.

Now as an online business owner, you most likely won't need a large team, and everyone might work remotely and connect virtually. You may find yourself working from home alone most of the time, which can make it hard to feel like you have actually achieved CEO status. But just remember each and every one of those steps that you climbed up your ladder that have brought you to this point. It's not that a CEO neglects the details, it's just that they've worked hard to build a highly motivated team of people who take care of the details and make meaningful contributions to help your company achieve the goals that you've defined.

In the end, I think one of the most important things to remember as you're climbing your ladder, reaching up for that top rung, is that everybody's ladder is different. Everyone climbs at different paces, and if you need to move up and down your ladder at some particular time to manage an issue don't worry about what it looks like to the outside world. Just do what you need to do to keep your ladder stable. Being agile is one of the best skills that you can have in a business because it means that as change happens, and it will happen, you can fix things fast and continue to grow.

PART 4

Troubleshooting

Success is not final;
failure is not fatal:
It is the courage to
continue that counts.

Winston S. Churchill

18

When You Fall Off Your Ladder

Sometimes in our businesses, we make decisions that don't turn out the way we had hoped. Or maybe life happens and your business has to take a back burner. Don't get too upset with yourself. There are plenty of amazingly successful entrepreneurs that have at one point in their career, fallen off their ladder and had to dust themselves off and get back up. Maybe they had to step away from their business. Perhaps they went bankrupt and decided to take what they learned from that experience and move forward to start a new business. There are a plethora of examples I could give that would show that a lot of entrepreneurs have been knocked down at least once in their career.

Don't fret. This doesn't mean you can't succeed. Falling off your ladder or slipping down a rung or two, might happen from time to time. What we want to do is quickly get back up, learn from our experience, and take that with us to help us climb even higher, or to secure a more sustainable spot at the top of our ladder.

Now, what are some ways that we know we may have been falling down our ladder? First off, if you're not able to sell, and you start to have to let people that work for you go, and now you are required to assume lower roles within your organization, that may be an indicator that you've fallen off just a little bit, but that doesn't mean you can't bounce back. Sometimes going lean in your business is exactly what you need to help it grow.

Remember that just because people have filled spots in lower rungs within your organization, doesn't mean that things can't change. Sometimes roles need to be merged. Sometimes you need to pare down and create a smaller team to take your business to the next level.

Bigger isn't necessarily always better. In fact, you should always be reviewing the overhead of your business and the cash flow of your business, to ensure that it can sustainably grow. It's tough to keep a business ladder together if you aren't bringing in cash to ensure that it stays stable. And you can't move up your ladder if you aren't making the income required to do so.

So keep in mind that paring down when needed us an efficient and smart way to move your business forward and is a sure sign that you are embodying that CEO role within your organization.

CEOs have to make tough decisions sometimes, but that doesn't mean you've fallen down your ladder. Making those decisions consciously and prudently says that you have achieved CEO status like a Rockstar.

Now actually falling off your ladder… believe me, you'll know the feeling, hitting each rung as you go down. It's like big mistakes that you may have made, that you can look back at and you say, "Holey Moley, why did I do that? What in the world was I thinking?"

In my life, I have had a few things happen personally that at the time, just made me incapable of selling. It just made me not want to get out there into the world and talk. So what did I do? I stopped selling. You know what I didn't do? I didn't pare down my team. I didn't cut expenses. That means I was still paying the salaries, the bills, but I certainly wasn't bringing in as much money, and that really hurt. It pushed me down on my ladder at least a few rungs and I was forced to tighten up my expenses until I was able to start selling again. I needed to understand how my personal life was affecting my business life, learn from my mistakes, get some good coaching, and move forward.

Do I feel bad about it? Sure.

Do I feel like I could have avoided it? Maybe.

Do I feel like I can do anything about what's past? No.

The only thing that you can do when you fall down your ladder is get back up and climb again. You have the choice to get angry at yourself for making the mistake in the first place, or you can learn from the experience and use it to become a better CEO.

There is no way to avoid making mistakes. That's what it is to be human. You can try to run a perfect business, but we live in an imperfect world with imperfect people, and mistakes are bound to happen. Some will be your fault, some will be your team's fault, some will be your client's fault, and some will just be the world's fault. The truth is that it doesn't matter whose fault it is. If you want to be successful then you don't waste time trying to place blame. The successful entrepreneur gets back up, takes ownership no matter what, and keeps on climbing.

19

When You Feel Like You Picked the Wrong Ladder

Are you starting to get that nagging feeling that maybe you picked the wrong ladder? It may be just a passing feeling, or it could be an accurate indicator that you need to move on.

Now, there's a difference between feeling like you picked the wrong ladder because you're just not able to get the business to work and become profitable, and feeling like you've built the wrong ladder, because you're just unhappy and hate what you're doing. Those are two very different things, and we should talk about both.

Number one, if you are just not able to get the business to work, you've read through this whole book, and you're realizing you're still at intern phase, or still at the janitor phase, and no matter what you're trying, nothing is working. Maybe your product or service you is just not selling.

This may mean that you need to bring a coach in to assess the situation. Maybe there are one or two things that you could do to make it better. Maybe you need an expert to help you get the traction in that particular area of business that isn't working.

I can't tell you when you should abandon your ladder and find a new one, or build a new one. That's something for you to decide. But you do need to understand your opportunity cost.

Opportunity cost is the price you pay for sticking around in a losing situation for too long. You end up losing out on the potential opportunities because you are using up your resources in the wrong places.

If you're working in a business that's just not working, and you can't get it to work, then you're losing the opportunity to be building something else that might work. I remember when I first quit my job and started my own business back in 2013. I thought I wanted to be a mindful communication coach because I wanted to pursue my passion for communication. I believe I was good at mindful communication coaching and I loved teaching it, but while I was passionate about it, it turns out, it wasn't my gift. You know, that thing that I can do in a fraction of the time that everybody else can do it.

After a year of trying to make that work and making sporadic income, I finally realized, through a series of events, that I was in the wrong place trying to climb the wrong ladder. I was no longer passionate about the topic because it was a continual uphill battle to get clients. I had invested way too much money into a business that wasn't making me any money.

When I realized, through the help of a friend, that my gift was really in content strategy, understanding how to structure your business for success, and how to attract clients, I was able to start generating income faster. Eureka! I had found my new ladder, and that ladder was built and climbed so much faster.

Now, second, what if you aren't happy anymore? It happens a lot more than you would think. You might climb one ladder, find a new passion and decide to build something new.

First assess whether or not you need to build a new ladder, or if you can simply alter the one you are on right now. There are so many situations where you might decide the best strategy is to make alterations in your existing business.

1. It may be that your kids are getting to a certain age where you want to hang out with them more.

2. It may be that you really, really used to love selling in your business and you wanted to embody that role, and now you're just not enjoying it as much.

Either way, my biggest recommendation is that you find somebody who is farther along than you to talk through your situation and goals. Tell them why you're not happy. Tell them what it is that you're doing in your business that doesn't serve you anymore. Tell them what you're longing for and what you wish you could be doing. It may be a situation where a few simple changes can be made to shift your business enough to reinvigorate your passion. Find somebody you trust and respect, and talk it out.

Whatever you decide, I want you to know that you are not alone. Tons of successful entrepreneurs will tell you that they tried out several ideas before the right one stuck. Pivoting is not a bad thing, as long as you take the time to assess the situation and make sure that you aren't pivoting simply because you haven't given your first ladder the time it needed to succeed.

20

When You Are Scared to Move Up

If you are afraid to move up your ladder, I completely understand. Making decisions in your business can be scary. It can be scary to delegate. It can be scary to create automation and spend money to get things done. I really do understand; I have been there.

Here's the thing. You can't be an island. You can't build the business that you want to build all by yourself. You need tools, you need automation. you need systems, and you're going to need people at some point. Whether those people are mentors or guides to help pull you up to the top, or whether those are team members that help push you up from the bottom, you will need people to help you succeed.

If you don't climb your ladder, then your business will not be sustainable. That's just a fact. As you grow in your business, things will change. Your experiences will change. Your knowledge will change. You will be in demand, and you will realize to grow you need to expand. Don't fight it. Allow it to happen. Get the support you need when you need it.

You decided to create a ladder in the first place, and that is a lot of responsibility to shoulder. I know it can be scary to help make things succeed. Believe me, there are tons of talks, articles, books that speak to the idea that it's just as scary to succeed as it is to fail. You're not alone in what you're feeling right now. If growing a business were easy, everyone would be an entrepreneur. You have decided to start something amazing, and it's your job to see it through.

My friend, Jen Rosenbaum, said, "Run towards the pain," and I encourage you to do that right now. If you can hold the hand of somebody you trust and listen to those around you who you respect, it makes that process so much easier. Make sure that your fear of climbing your ladder isn't keeping you from getting all the things you want, all the support you need, and building the life and the business that will make you satisfied and happy.

21

Stop Looking at Other People's Ladders

I'm not gonna sugarcoat it; sometimes we can't look away when it comes to looking at another business owner's success (particularly if it's a competitor). It's just so in our face that it becomes a legitimate distraction. And even if we don't realize it, that break in focus on our own goals and progress can become a major setback.

I remember back when I was first getting started...

There was one business in particular that started gaining steam in my market and went from relatively unknown, to micro-celebrity overnight, and I found myself looking on in wonder.

"What are they doing that I'm not?"

"What have they got that I don't?"

It was a weird mix of jealousy and intrigue, resentment and awe. It's not that I didn't want this other business to succeed - I've always believed there's enough business for everyone and that 'a rising tide raises all ships' - but it was more like I just couldn't figure out what was so magical about their brand that was drawing everyone in so quickly.

In spite of my best effort to stay focused on my own budding business, I found myself poring over their marketing (it was oh-so polished), saving their emails (beautifully copy-written and ultra-consistent), and wondering what I was doing wrong.

The truth is, I wasn't doing anything wrong. Other than wasting time looking at someone else's ladder that is.

Even though my perception was that we were at the same level, I found out later that we weren't. I'd only been in business for a year, and the other company had been at it - struggling - for the better part of 5 years before they finally caught their "break."

What's crazy is that when you start talking to successful business owners, they almost always have some version of the same story. The "overnight success" you see was ten years in the making, and everything they did up until their star was born was precisely what they had to do to be ready for success when it showed up.

Every single setback they had faced along the way gave them the experience they needed to move to the next level.

Boss Mom took off a couple of months later, and before long I was too busy trying to figure out how to deal with the influx of new subscribers, students, and clients to pay much attention to what anyone else's business was doing.

So what's the best remedy when someone else's ladder is pulling you away from your own?

Truthfully? It's getting into massive action and creating momentum by staying laser-focused on your mission. It's setting your proverbial sails on a specific course, breaking down the steps you need to take to get there, and then checking off those boxes as you complete those steps.

Author Napoleon Hill wrote in his now famous Think & Grow Rich (published in 1937) "Definiteness of Purpose is the starting point of all achievement. Decide what you want, find out how to get it, and then take daily action toward achieving your goal. Successful people move on their initiative, but they know where they are going before they start."

It's hard to worry about what other people are doing when you're working your system. When you're taking purposeful steps toward building the business you envision.

Remember that writing your to-do list the evening before you plan to do it allows your subconscious mind to find ways to accomplish your tasks faster, better, smarter so that each day you wake up ready to dive straight into action.

Armed with your list each morning, you get to seize the day right from the very start. Throw yourself into those tasks you know will have the most significant impact before you do anything else. Avoid social media and email until those tasks are complete. That way it will be impossible to allow yourself to get distracted until you've knocked out your most crucial to-dos.

Then, if you want to allow yourself the space to creep on your competition, maybe lament for a minute that you aren't going fast enough, you'll already have taken steps that day to move up the ladder.

Are there going to be peers who appear to be passing you along the way? Definitely. Is it going to be an annoying distraction that has you questioning your direction, ability, and purpose? Probably.

But if you can keep your eyes looking up – to that incredible outcome you envisioned for yourself when you started - and keep moving stoically toward it (even when it feels like nothing is happening) you'll eventually notice how high you have climbed.

And, at that moment, if you look around (just for a second), you'll probably notice people are watching you, wondering how the heck you got to where you are "overnight."

22

Always Remember the Climb

Tim Fargo famously said, "who you are tomorrow begins with who you are today." You don't have to start at the top to get to the top. Pretty much every single person that 'rose to greatness' did just that, they 'rose' one step at a time.

Embrace the step that you are on at this moment. Use this book as a field guide to help you see where you are and when it's time to move up. Leverage your community, and your support system.

I saw a great quote from the Chicago Tribune that said, "who, exactly seeks out a coach?...winners who want even more out of life." Every single successful entrepreneur that I have met has told me that they would have never succeeded without the help of the coaches they hired along the way. When you can't seem to figure out your next step, get someone to help you keep moving.

And finally, get up every single day and recognize that you have chosen to build something amazing. Climbing your own ladder takes time and effort and you have decided to jump in and change the world anyway. You are the future; so thank you for all you do and for all you will do.

Now go out and keep climbing and I'll see you at the top.

ACKNOWLEDGEMENTS

Thank you, first and foremost to my mom and step-father. Every single time I get asked how I got to where I am today I answer, without hesitation, that I was loved so greatly and challenged so graciously that I know I am worthy of love, and can weather any storm. Those two qualities are the best gifts any parent can give.

To Dawn Marrs, Kelsey Murphy and Natalie Gingrich, these women make me feel loved and valued and also make me laugh. If you don't have friends that call you randomly on a Tuesday just to remind you that you are amazing and contribute to the world in a unique way, then you need to go find someone like one of these ladies. They will change your life.

To Ryan Malstaff, who is an amazing role model for our children. I feel eternally lucky to have him as the father of our children.

To Samantha Johnston and Amy Lockrin, my work-wives. These two women have such brilliant minds and are so fiercely loyal in their work ethic and their friendship that I wake up every morning wondering how on earth I got so lucky.

To Matt Johnson who broadened my perspective and challenged my ideas in all the best ways. This book would not exist as it is without his input.

To Valerie Friedlander, my life coach, who has helped me grow and be a better person. Everyone needs a life-coach.

To Carrie Clark and Maria Desmondy, my mastermind ladies, the world is a better place for having these two brilliant, funny, and kind ladies in it.

To Julie Ball, CEO of Sparkle Hustle Grow, who is the most beautiful example of how collaboration over competition will actually make you more successful.

To Mike Keonigs, who has such a giving heart and has been such an amazing mentor these past two years.

ABOUT THE AUTHOR

Dana is Mom to two amazing kids who already associate 'work' with doing things you love that make the world a better place.

She started the Boss Mom Movement in 2015 after starting her business and immediately getting pregnant, which led her to write her first book, *Boss Mom.* Since then, Dana has been named one of the top 50 female entrepreneurs to watch  out for in 2017 by the Huffington Post, and has been featured by Fast Company, Inc., Social Media Examiner, Smart Passive Income and many more.

Dana has embraced every step on her own business ladder and leveraged what she learned to help thousands of women start, grow, and scale their online businesses.

TO LEARN MORE ABOUT DANA, GO TO:

WWW.BOSS-MOM.COM/ABOUT

DANA IS A PROUD SUPPORTER & LEAGUE MEMBER OF THE JUST LIKE MY CHILD FOUNDATION

The Just Like My Child Foundation (JLMC) has delivered healthcare services, education, microenterprise, social justice, leadership and empowerment programs to over 200,000 individuals (primarily women and children) in 76 rural communities in Central Uganda and Senegal.

After more than a decade of experience, JLMC developed the Girl Power Project® so they could equip girls with the tools, skills, and attitudes to stay in school and avoid early pregnancy and disease. Their mission is to empower vulnerable adolescent girls by enabling them to create healthy, self-sustaining families who prosper without further aid.

By purchasing this book you have already contributed to the Just Like My Child Foundation, and if you want to make and even bigger impact you can find out how to join the League at www.JustLikeMyChild.org

Made in the USA
San Bernardino, CA
28 October 2018